KYN

KNOW YOUR NUMBERS
KNOW YOUR BUSINESS

MASTERING CASH FLOW

How Business Owners Can Banish Stress & Sleepless Nights, And Secure Funding For Growth!

Take a few seconds and imagine never worrying about cash flow again.

What would that do for your business and for you personally?

If you adopt these key cash flow optimisation strategies in this book, you will reduce stress and never have a sleepless night again. PLUS you will also understand how to secure the funding required for growth.

CRAIG ALEXANDER RATTRAY

COPYRIGHT © 2023
CRAIG ALEXANDER RATTRAY

All rights reserved. Without limiting the rights under copyright reserved above, no part of this book may be reproduced, stored or introduced into a retrieval system, or transmitted, in any form or by any means (electronic, mechanical, photocopying, recording or otherwise), without the prior written permission of both the copyright owner and the publisher.

Published by Craig Alexander Rattray Limited.

DISCLAIMER

This book contains the opinions and ideas of the author. The purpose of this book is to provide you with helpful information about managing cash flow in your business. This book should not be relied upon solely to improve cash flow in your business. Careful attention has been paid to ensure the accuracy of the information, but the author cannot assume responsibility for the validity or consequences of its use. This information is not intended to be all things to all businesses. It is, by nature, generic, to most businesses in general.

The material in this book is for informational purposes only. As each individual situation is unique, the author claims no responsibility for any adverse effects that may result from using or applying the information in this book. Any use of the information found in this book is the sole responsibility of the reader. Any suggestions found in this book are to be followed only after consultation with your own business advisors.

DEDICATION

This book is dedicated to the ambitious men and women who have started their own businesses and struggle along with limited help from accountants and finance professionals.

MY MISSION

My mission is to assist business owners and allow them to better understand their numbers and cash flow to allow them to make better decisions thereby increasing profitability, cash flow and shareholder value, whilst at the same time reducing stress.

MY TWO RULES FOR RUNNING YOUR BUSINESS

RULE #1:
FOCUS ON CASH

RULE #2:
NEVER FORGET RULE #1

Craig Alexander Rattray

WELCOME AND THANK YOU

Thank you for investing in your copy of Know Your Numbers: Mastering Cash Flow. I believe that cash flow management can be taught and mastered. The purpose of this book (and the related resources) is to allow you to do just that.

TAKE OUR FREE ONLINE CASH FLOW DIAGNOSTIC SCORECARD

I have created a simple diagnostic scorecard to help you understand the cash flow risk that's inherent in your business. It only takes a couple of minutes but will give you an incredibly valuable insight into your business.

You can take the diagnostic at:

kyncashflowdiagnostic.com

KNOW YOUR NUMBERS MASTERING CASH FLOW

How Business Owners Can Banish Stress & Sleepless Nights, And Secure Funding For Growth!

> Adopt Key Cash Flow Optimisation Strategies And You Will <u>NEVER</u> Have Stress Or Sleepless Nights Again!
>
> **Craig Alexander Rattray**

TABLE OF Contents

WHO SHOULD READ THIS BOOK?	1
INTRODUCTION	6
FINANCIAL MANAGEMENT	16
CASH INFLOWS	26
CASH OUTFLOWS	36
FINANCING GROWTH	44
BANKS AND INVESTORS	49
KEY PERFORMANCE INDICATORS (KPIs) AND RATIOS	56
CASH FLOW MANAGEMENT MYTHS	60
ROLLING CASH FORECASTS	65
THE NEXT STEP	73

APPENDICES

CASH FLOW DIAGNOSTIC SCORECARD	74
RECOMMENDED READING	75
THE KYN LEARNING ACADEMY	75
ROLLING CASH FLOW EXAMPLE	76
CASE STUDIES	78
ABOUT THE AUTHOR	**86**
GLOSSARY	**87**

WHO SHOULD READ THIS BOOK?

I have been involved in starting, running, managing, investing in, and advising businesses for more than three decades.

I understand the challenges of owning and running a business and the impact that it has on each business owner, their mindset, and their family and personal relationships.

A Google search of "what keeps business owners awake at night" produces over 2 billion results.

If you review the first few pages of these results, cash flow and cash management are the biggest challenges facing businesses.

Business owners worry about many things, but cash flow is by far their top concern. Do you ever lie awake at night asking yourself one or more of these questions?

- How do I pay my employees at the end of the week or month?
- How do I pay my suppliers?
- How do I fund the stock I need to hold to satisfy my customer orders?
- Why does it take us so long to issue sales invoices?
- Why do my customers take so long to pay me?
- How do I finance the growth opportunities?
- How do I pay myself?
- How do I fund my retirement?
- How do I raise working capital?
- Why won't my bank help me?
- Why won't my accountant help me with these questions?

These questions, and many more, keep business owners awake at night. I have been there and face similar questions from clients and business owners daily.

However, by reading and implementing the advice in this short book I believe that these problems can be resolved, and you, the business owner, will know how to address them before they become insurmountable.

I believe that cash flow can always be improved, and that cash management can be taught and mastered.

There have been numerous studies conducted over the years globally and it remains the biggest issue for business owners and the thing that keeps business owners like you awake at night.

Cash Flow Worries! Sadly, you are not alone….

- A Fin Pacific study stated that "69% of business owners report having sleepless nights over their cash flow". Be honest with yourself, have cash flow issues ever kept you awake at night?

- US Bank study stated that 83% of business failures cited poor cash management as a key factor (Dryrun.com).

- In "QuickBooks State of Cash Flow Report", of the 44% of businesses that ran out of money, nearly half were taken completely by surprise.

- With more than 30 million business owners in the USA, DaySmart Software says cash flow is the number one challenge for small businesses. According to the data, making enough money keeps 54% of small business owners up at night which tops the five challenges facing small businesses in their report.

- American Express published research that nearly half of business owners in the UK believe that poor cash flow is stopping their business from reaching its full potential and 56 per cent feel that the challenges associated with poor cash flow prevent them from making growth decisions. A further 25 per cent said poor cash flow keeps them awake at night, while 24 per cent of Small – Medium Sized Enterprise owners feel stress in their personal lives for the same reason. In the UK there are almost 6 million SMEs representing 99% of all businesses.

- Nearly 30% of all businesses will die due to cash flow issues, yet according to a study by Intuit, 83% of businesses owners possessed a basic or failing grade of financial literacy. Intuit asked businesses for input beyond cash flow shortfalls and fear. They asked them about growth. 76% of business owners are worried that cash flow issues will affect growth.

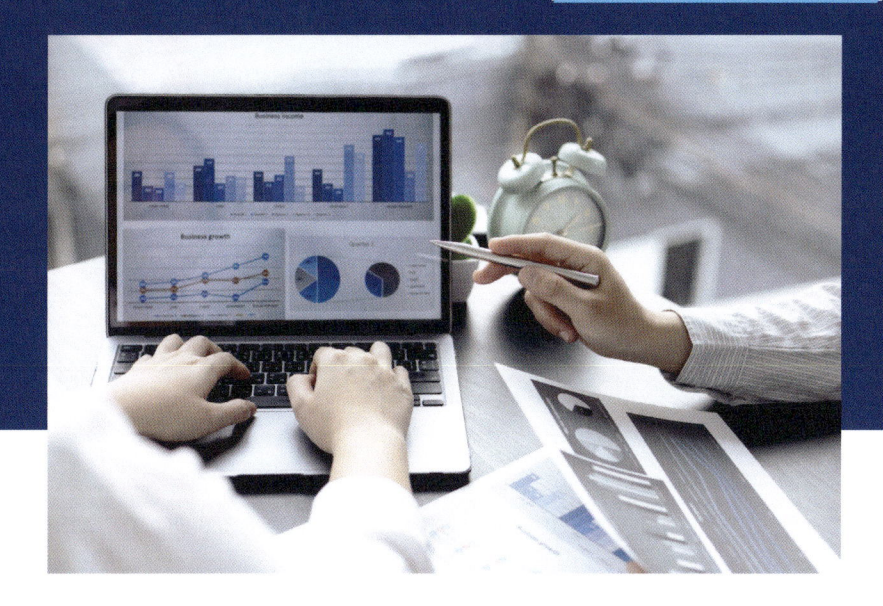

This book aims to tip the balance and help business owners in the cash flow fight by improving their understanding and their level of financial literacy, as well as the core issue of cash flow management.

During my time working with hundreds of businesses over the years I have experienced the frustration of business owners like you. As a business owner, I have been there too.

I have been in many situations where I have worried about paying bills and the lack of cash.

I have worried about how to pay myself and pay my taxes on time.

However, I have learned from all of that and have acted and created systems, methodologies and tips, courses, and Mastermind Groups, that I use with my clients and in my own companies daily.

I often say "adopt key cash flow optimisation strategies, and you will NEVER have a sleepless night again!"

I genuinely believe that.

This book is for you – the business owner who wants to run their business and sleep soundly at night knowing everything is taken care of from a cash perspective.

The information and concepts outlined are not particularly new or ground-breaking. In many cases, they are sensible and should be obvious to many finance professionals. I want them to become obvious and automatic for you, the business owner, too.

I promise that if you read this book, follow the guidance, and apply the tips and suggestions then you will never have another sleepless night over cash flow.

I would go so far as stating that if you read this, adopt the learnings, and your cash flow still causes you sleepless nights, then I will refund the cost of the book (as long as your business is profitable).

I look forward to making your business-owning journey a much more pleasant and less stressful experience.

INTRODUCTION

In my experience, most accountants and business owners do not fully understand cash flow and how to make it better. That is a bold statement.

Those accountants that do understand cash flow are often too busy dealing with other historic matters like prior year accounts and tax returns to think about looking forward and to advise their clients about cash flow. Many business owners do not consider asking their accountant to assist with cash flow or with forward looking matters.

WHAT IS CASH FLOW?

Simply, cash flow is the flow of cash into and out of your business bank account.

Cash flow should be thought of in a similar way to fuel in your car or oxygen in the atmosphere – run out of fuel and the car stops, run out of oxygen and we die.

Michael Dell, founder and CEO, Dell Technologies commented:
"We were always focused on our profit and loss statement. But cash flow was not a regularly discussed topic. It was as if we were driving along, watching only the speedometer, when in fact we were running out of gas."

It goes without saying that all businesses should aim for positive cash flow by generating more cash (inflows) than they are spending (outflows).

The best way to do that is to have a profitable business, and to understand the many and varied cash flows and their timings.

The Intuit whitepaper, "QuickBooks State of Cash Flow Report", states that 62% of all businesses admit to experiencing a cash flow shortfall, or nearly running out of money.

WHAT IS CASH FLOW MANAGEMENT?

Quite simply cash flow management is a set of procedures, policies and actions that allow a business owner to track, understand and improve cash flow.

Any business owner must understand the cash inflows, the cash outflows, and the precise cash position on an ongoing basis. That is the key to effective cash flow management.

By preparing in advance with cash flow management, shortfalls can be highlighted, action taken, and the business can continue to trade on a satisfactory basis whilst keeping all suppliers and employees happy and paid on time.

Successful cash flow management predicts cash inflows, cash outflows and the future cash position whether that is an excess or a shortfall.

According to a study by Fin Pacific, businesses managing their cash flow monthly have an 80% survival rate versus businesses that rely on cash flow planning as an annual activity. That percentage increases by managing cash flow daily or even weekly.

After many years of dealing with frustrated business owners suffering many of the same problems, I wanted to turn my experience to helping you, the business owner.

This book is for you:
- the business owner who wants to sleep at night and have a strong positive cash flow.
- the business owner who wants cash to be managed effectively, efficiently, and effortlessly.
- the business owner who wants to pay employees, suppliers, and taxes on time without stress.

I know that business owners worry about cash flow. I see it and experience it every day.

It is the thing I am asked about most often.

WHY IS CASH IMPORTANT?

Many business owners fail to understand that there is a difference between profit and cash.

If you own a profitable business and were paid for all sales immediately you would never have a cash flow problem. However, as we all know most businesses make sales and provide credit terms so whilst the sale is made today, the cash may not be received for 30 days or more.

No business can survive without cash (or adequate bank facilities).

If your company is making losses, then it will inevitably consume cash, so the starting point is to ensure that you have a profitable business. That falls outside the scope of this book and is something I will revisit in a future book.

For this book's purposes it is assumed that you own a profitable business.

WHAT DOES IT MEAN TO OWN A PROFITABLE BUSINESS?

Profit is the difference between the total of all sales less the total of all costs and expenses for a particular period.

Many business owners may realise at some stage that that the profit they make in the business does not equal their cash flow, unless they are dealing solely in cash which is unlikely today.

However, even profitable businesses cannot survive without cash – as I said earlier, think of cash as the oxygen a business needs to stay alive.

A sale can be made today generating the profit, but the cash may not be received for perhaps 30 days or more. How do you fund the costs during that intervening period? You probably have employees to pay; rent on premises; materials and other costs used to generate the sale; and other business overheads. Please never forget sales tax and corporate taxes which will fall due later.

It is vital to understand timings of cash flow both in and out.

If that is all true and important, then why does everyone not forecast cash flow?

That is the key question.

In my view it is madness not to.

However, most businesses do not actively manage their cash flow.

If in doubt, remember the phrase "**cash is king**" – like most popular phrases, it has been created for a reason and I believe it is true.

A similar saying is that "revenue is vanity, profit is sanity and cash flow is reality". Also true.

I have never encountered a successful business that does not actively manage their cash flow, and similarly I have never come across a failing business that did actively manage their cash flow before it was too late.

Whilst some business owners do not want to know or do not have the time to actively manage their cash flow, I believe that the biggest reason is that you, the business owner, do not know where to start and do not properly understand cash flow.

Managing cash flow can also help you and your management team identify problems in the business faster than any other diagnostic tool.

It should also be remembered that the value of a business is dependent on cash flow, not solely profits.

My aim in this book is to give you the missing knowledge and to suggest some useful tools to allow you to forecast and manage cash flow.

I believe that with a little help, some advice and pointing in the right direction, that all business owners can master cash flow.

I will go through this in more detail, but for now, here are five introductory key tips to enhance and improve cash flow and cash management:

- Ensure your financial information is up to date.
- Prepare a rolling 13-week cash flow forecast using a spreadsheet or app add-in like Dryrun or Float.
- Update the forecast weekly as a minimum; daily is easier and preferable.
- Keep sales tax, employee taxes and corporate taxes due in a separate bank account. Remember it is not your money.
- Ensure you have a cash "buffer" or adequate working capital facilities that have been pre-arranged with your bank or finance provider.

A study from Fin Pacific stated that 70% of businesses that fail were profitable when they ceased trading.

So why did they fail? **Cash Flow.**

These businesses failed to match their cash outflows with cash inflows and did not have an adequate cash buffer or working capital facility.

How could that be avoided? Simple.

1. Better cash management;
2. Use of real-time historic financial information; and,
3. Good forecasts, particularly a weekly rolling cash flow model, showing the peaks and troughs over the forthcoming period.

If you do not measure cash flow, you will not be able to manage it effectively and make the right decisions.

Without that tool, you may well spend the money this week that you need the following week.

How will you know that without a weekly forecast?

Cash flow management and planning reduces stress and improves your chances of success. It puts the business owner in control of an area that many business owners neglect.

Remember, cash flow worries are the biggest area that keeps business owners awake at night.

I can guarantee that effective cash management will make the future even brighter than the past and will mean lots of restful nights with no cash worries.

Three key points to remember throughout this book:

1. If you do not make a profit you will not generate positive cash flow from trading.
2. Without up-to-date historic figures, your current cash position, and a forecast, you will never be able to manage cash flow optimally and effectively.
3. Cash is king.

NEED HELP?

Knowing where to start is the most critical step in your cash flow journey. Your cash flow can best be analysed and improved with the help of a trusted adviser. I work with many companies and help them improve their cash flow.

At Know Your Numbers, we understand the difference between a thriving business and a struggling one is how well they manage their finances. When you join Know Your Numbers Mastery, you will be taught how to master your finances and how to **apply** those learnings in your business.

Make better decisions, feel more confident and less stressed, and have a thriving business.

Learn more here: **knowyournumbers.biz/**

HOW DOES THIS APPLY TO ME?

Before you move on, take a moment to reflect upon what you have learned in this chapter. What are the three most important "golden nuggets" you can apply in your business today?

_____
_____
_____
_____
_____
_____
_____
_____

FINANCIAL MANAGEMENT

Whilst this book focuses on cash flow and cash management, it is inextricably linked to Financial Management.

As the business owner you are not expected to be the finance expert.
However, you must understand your financials and your cash flow. You must know your numbers.

Many business owners who have run their own company for many years are often too proud to admit they do not fully understand accounts and finance.

Do not be one of them!

Bring in people to help you who understand accounts and finance either full-time, part-time or on an outsourced basis. It is possible to outsource all parts of the finance function and the requirements will vary depending on your company size, business sector and stage of development.

Then, ask lots of questions.
Understand what the numbers mean.
More importantly, understand the key numbers for YOUR business.

It is not difficult, and you do not need to be a rocket scientist to understand.

I have taught many business owners over the years to better understand and know their numbers thereby allowing them to make better decisions. It never ceases to surprise me the changes in business owners after they do this, and the usual comment – "it's not as difficult as I thought".

It is important to take financial management seriously and not to avoid personal responsibility. It is your business.

I believe in real time historic information and up-to-date integrated forecasts.
Without both, business owners and management teams are running blind.

How can effective and appropriate decisions be made without knowing the full financial picture?

Excellent financial management is about understanding:
- where you are
- where you have been
- where you are going

This is done by having:
- current management accounts and information, plus an up-to-date bank position – "where you are"
- historic management accounts and full-year final accounts – "where you have been"
- forecasts comprising monthly profit and loss, balance sheet and cash flow as well as a weekly rolling cash flow forecast – "where you are going"

These are your map and dashboard. Think of driving your car or flying a plane.

If you do not have the map and the dashboard then you will be lost and are unlikely to reach your targeted destination – and that is assuming you know where you want to go as many businesses do not have a strategic plan either.

Ensuring the company has timely historic financial information, well thought through strategic forecasts and a complete understanding of the cash position going forward is your very own dashboard which gives you the visibility and the route map required for the journey. The cash is the fuel to take you on the journey.

Do not meander aimlessly and without a plan.

So, what does that mean and what does that look like?

Good financial management means having all financial matters up to date with related reports, statistics, information, and Key Performance Indicators (KPIs). This comprises historic information, forecast information and usually an online/cloud accounting system.

Many years ago, there was little choice but to record every transaction manually. Now you can take advantage of advancements in technology whether storing spreadsheets in the cloud for easy access for multiple people, using software add-ins that process invoices and linking that with cloud accounting software.

I cannot recommend having an online software solution highly enough. It saves time, is more accurate and if managed daily, the company can have real-time financial information.

In a study by UK based Financial Director, 34% of finance leaders stated that their team relied on manual expense or invoice processes even though they were "hugely time consuming and archaic." Deloitte's 2020 report "Accelerate Digitalisation" found that "digital processes are key to building resilience in the face of disastrous world events, such as the Coronavirus pandemic." It encouraged companies to rethink and accelerate their digitisation strategy.

I agree – do it – go digital.

I am a great believer in the "if you do everything every day you are only ever a day behind" approach. Online accounting software makes this much easier than manual accounting or the "old" days of using a system that was only on one computer.

It is assumed that all businesses are using electronic banking for payments and receipts. Please try to avoid the use of paper cheques as they are cumbersome and take up administration time to process, bank and deal with generally, as well as occasionally being rejected due to insufficient funds in the payer's account – this then takes up more administration time.

Doing everything every day means:
- Complete all bank reconciliations
- Issue sales invoices for completed work, services or products sold
- Process purchase invoices
- Chase overdue payments
- Process any other cash related matters and update the cash flow forecast with any future commitments

A report by the UK Turnaround Management Society stated that 36% of business failures are caused by inadequate financial management.

U.S. Bank conducted a study and discovered that 82% of the time, poor business cash flow management or poor understanding of cash flow contributes to the failure of a small business.

In QuickBooks "State of Cash Flow Report", 44% of businesses that ran out of money, nearly half were taken completely by surprise.

Cash flow should never be a surprise if it is managed regularly and effectively.

Become a part of the minority who carefully plan and manage cash flow. A Geneva Business Bank study suggests 68% of small businesses performed no cash flow analysis. It goes further to state that businesses only planning once a year have a 36% survival rate over 5 years, meaning two out of every three businesses will go out of business, while those planning monthly have an 80% survival rate.

I maintain that cash flow management is not difficult and by following a series of simple steps on a regular basis that it can be mastered.

The purpose of this book is to inform, educate and guide you as the business owner on that cash mastery journey.

My initial discussions with business owners when working on finance related roles have always been to understand what they know about accounts and finance, and more importantly to educate them on the interaction between the different accounting reports. This aids not only understanding but improves the likelihood of making optimal decisions and that they understand the impacts of such decisions.

These insights are key to managing, forecasting, and driving the business forward.

"If you can't measure it, you can't improve it." A quote attributed to Peter Drucker.

Seems sensible.

"I would go further and state that, if you do not measure it, you cannot manage it. If it is not measured, where is the accountability?

Measurement and accountability go hand-in-hand.

Too many businesses do not manage the important things.

That can vary between businesses, business sectors and stages of development.

However, there is one constant that should be managed regardless of size, stage, or sector.

Cash, including a review of actuals for the previous week and actuals against forecast to understand what was different and how that impacts on the forecast going forward.

Responsibility MUST be allocated to someone to measure it, monitor it, and forecast it.

I would go so far to say that if there is only one thing measured in a company well, make it cash.

Key tips for effective financial management:

1. Have an effective and accountable finance person/team (in-house or outsourced) that produces good quality and timely information
2. Understand your figures
3. Use an online accounting software system
4. Update your accounting records daily
5. Review regularly – weekly at a minimum for cash flow, and monthly for management accounts comprising monthly and year-to-date profit and loss, balance sheet and cash flow reports, and related variance reports comparing actual against budget/forecast.

As a business owner it is important to have a plan of where you want to get to. Are you planning to grow the business? Are you working towards exit and handover to your family? Are you thinking of selling in three years?

Whatever it is, ensure that you have a clear strategic plan. Then you can prepare a forecast to ensure you understand how much cash you need to carry it out. I discuss Financing Growth in a subsequent chapter.

NEED HELP?

Knowing where to start is the most critical step in your cash flow journey. Your cash flow can best be analysed and improved with the help of a trusted adviser. I work with many companies and help them improve their cash flow.

At Know Your Numbers, we understand the difference between a thriving business and a struggling one is how well they manage their finances. When you join Know Your Numbers Mastery, you will be taught how to master your finances and how to **apply** those learnings in your business.

Make better decisions, feel more confident and less stressed, and have a thriving business.

Learn more here: **knowyournumbers.biz/**

HOW DOES THIS APPLY TO ME?

Before you move on, take a moment to reflect upon what you have learned in this chapter. What are the three most important "golden nuggets" you can apply in your business today?

_____
_____
_____
_____
_____
_____
_____
_____
_____

CASH INFLOWS

Typically, cash inflows are generated from sales to customers (trade receivables or trade debtors).

Please remember that a sale is not a sale until the cash is in your bank account.

Inflows may also come from asset sales, new loans, grants or investment.

In general, we want to speed up cash inflows.

This is vitally important as delays in payment from customers are the biggest factor in poor cash flow.

According to the 2020 QuickBooks Cash Flow survey, between 2018 and 2019 small businesses averaged an 81% increase in outstanding receivables.

We know that late payments are rising. Fundbox analysed 20 million invoices and found that 64% of businesses are paid late. They found that 48% of net 30, 45% of net 60 and 35% of net 90 invoices resulted in late payments.

The SME Loans report "The Ultimate Guide to Managing Cash Flow" stated that 78% of UK SMEs are waiting one month beyond agreed credit terms before payment. 40% of UK SMEs claim that large businesses are the worst offenders.

What impact does that have on your business?

Work out how much of your potential cash you have tied-up in receivables over more than 30 days. What difference would that cash make to you if it were already in your bank account, not only now, but on an ongoing basis?

According to the 2020 QuickBooks "State of Payments" report, 62% of small business owners are unsure how much money is received into their bank account each month.

This is a surprising statistic. I want to change that and make you in the minority who do know and more importantly understand.

Credit terms and cash collection processes are a key part of good cash management.

I know from experience that effective credit control will result in improved receipts. Many businesses try to stretch payments as much as possible and await calls from suppliers to chase for payment. It is usually the supplier that chases for payment that is the one that is paid.

BACS Payment Schemes reported that 43% of SMEs spend £4.4 billion in administration costs alone in chasing late payments and 11% of SMEs employ someone to chase up payments.

Intuit QuickBooks 2019 report stated that 1 in 7 companies had been unable to pay employees due to late receipts from customers.

These statistics are unlikely to change significantly and indeed I expect them to become worse. As a business owner you can make changes and implement systems and processes in your business to be the company that people pay on time or indeed early.

Late payments not only damage the companies involved, but they can take their toll on the business owners personally with respect to their health and relationships.

How do we improve cash inflows from customers?

1. **Invoice faster** - As a starting point, we should invoice as soon as the work is done, services are provided, or products delivered. How frequently and when do you invoice? If not daily, why not? Why wait until the end of the month? That only delays the customer receiving the invoice, processing it, and waiting for the credit terms to expire before paying.

   Ensure all invoices have the correct details to avoid unnecessary delays – this includes the correct company name, address, sent to the correct person and outlining the work done or service provided.

   Be clear on credit terms and show the due date on the invoice for any avoidance of doubt. Issued invoices should be sent electronically and include bank details.

2. **Provide clear credit terms and due dates** - Do you provide credit terms? Are these confirmed in writing?

   If credit is being offered to customers, we encourage the use of a credit application. It is important to know who you are dealing with – remember it is not a sale until the cash is in your bank account. This could be a standard form emailed to each new customer or even better, downloaded from your company website.

It should request all the usual basic company information including full name, company number, details of directors, and anticipated trading levels as well as credit limit requested. The company can then be credit checked by one of the online credit reference agencies (and additionally, with two of its current suppliers by way of a reference) and a credit limit assigned. This can be added to the accounting system and certain flags highlighted when the customer starts to trade close to its limit or indeed goes above that. The customer can be notified of the credit limit, credit terms and provided with the full trading terms and conditions. This can assist if there is ever a dispute.

3. **Follow a clearly defined credit control policy** - What is your debt collection process?

   Automatic electronic reminders can be generated from most accounting systems.

   This can be followed up with credit control calls a few days before payments fall due. This not only builds up a relationship with a customer contact and is good customer service, but it creates a pattern that your customer knows you will chase for payment. That makes it more likely that they will pay on time in preference to those customers who do not follow such routines.

4. **Review the outstanding trade receivables and trade debtors schedule -** This should be reviewed weekly and if you have a dedicated person, they should be chasing and reminding customers daily.

   Review the ageing schedule and in particular the columns showing 30/60/90/120+. I like to ensure that there is an action for every invoice over 30 days and responsibility is allocated for resolving any issues. This makes for easy follow-up and review and I guarantee that it improves cash collection.

5. **Understand your days sales outstanding and the financial impact** - For example, if your credit terms are 30 days and the days outstanding are 65 there is a mismatch and a big problem. Why are your customers paying late? You must understand why and do something about it.

   Remember, a sale is not a sale until the cash is in your bank account. If a customer subsequently fails to pay, you lose not only the profit that has already been accounted for, but you also lose the cost of the product delivered or time incurred by your staff in providing the service.

How can customers pay you?
Online and electronic payments should be the standard method of receipt. It avoids delays and awaiting cheques clearing.

Accept multiple payment methods particularly credit cards as those customers who are struggling with cash flow issues often revert to credit cards as cash reserves and bank facilities are eroded.

Consider the use of online payment portals like Stripe and PayPal – you have the option of passing on the additional costs to your customer.

Some methods to improve cash inflows from customers include:

1. Automatic payments from customers who pay for an ongoing service or product. This "recurring revenue" is of huge value to any business and means the month always starts with some guaranteed sales and cash in the bank. I work with many clients to introduce a variety of recurring revenue models.
2. Up-front payments for new customers or those with a poor credit rating. Do not provide credit terms if there is uncertainty over the future payment from a customer.
3. Ask for deposits or partial payments in advance and/or staged payments as work progresses. In these situations, phase payments with a smaller final percentage and more earlier as often formal sign-off from a customer may be delayed for administrative reasons or because a customer knows that they need to make a large final payment. Avoid payment on approval and instead link it to delivery or other milestones under your control.
4. Incentivise early payments. Consider offering prompt payment discounts but remember the impact this may have on your margins as there is a cost of doing so. If you do, ensure you have compared the cost of the lost margin against the funding cost of the earlier receipt.

SOME OTHER USEFUL TIPS INCLUDE:

1. By building a relationship with a specific person at the customer, it makes it easier to chase for payment. It also makes them think twice before making late payments. If they only have a few thousand pounds left to pay suppliers and it is between your business and another where there is no relationship, in most cases you will be paid as a result of the relationship.
2. As part of your ongoing review process, also consider customer payment patterns. It is easy to identify those who pay on time and those who are late. However, if a customer is regularly late by a few days because they pay say every Friday, my advice is not to disrupt such payment patterns. Of more concern is the customer that pays on time then is late for a few payments then starts to slip and deteriorate. This is often a sign of a challenging cash flow issue and is a red warning flag.
3. Open a "number 2 bank account" and transfer all sales taxes that are included in receipts from customers – this is not your money and is only being held by you before payment is due. By keeping it separate you will have fewer issues when the time for payment falls due.

WHAT TO DO IF A CUSTOMER DOES NOT PAY ON TIME OR EXCEEDS THE CREDIT LIMIT IN PLACE?

1. If matters have been discussed between the two finance teams, escalate to a senior member of your customer's company in the first instance. Try to identify and understand the issues and try to find an amicable way of resolving matters.
2. Consider stopping services until payment is made and the customer is operating within agreed credit terms.
3. Arrange a payment plan whereby the customer pays a certain amount every week.
4. Consider stopping working with the customer completely.
5. Take legal enforcement action. This is always a last resort as it is time consuming, costly and in most cases is the end of the customer relationship.

Remember that cash inflows are usually more difficult to forecast as they are not within your control. Regular review of cash inflows will improve your knowledge, understanding and visibility and form a key part of cash flow mastery.

NEED HELP?

Knowing where to start is the most critical step in your cash flow journey. Your cash flow can best be analysed and improved with the help of a trusted adviser. I work with many companies and help them improve their cash flow.

At Know Your Numbers, we understand the difference between a thriving business and a struggling one is how well they manage their finances. When you join Know Your Numbers Mastery, you will be taught how to master your finances and how to **apply** those learnings in your business.

Make better decisions, feel more confident and less stressed, and have a thriving business.
Learn more here: **knowyournumbers.biz/**

HOW DOES THIS APPLY TO ME?

Before you move on, take a moment to reflect upon what you have learned in this chapter. What are the three most important "golden nuggets" you can apply in your business today?

_____
_____
_____
_____
_____
_____

CASH OUTFLOWS

Typically, cash outflows relate to payments to suppliers (also known as Trade Payables or Trade Creditors), employee wages and salaries, and taxation (employee taxes, sales taxes, and corporate taxes).

Other cash outflows include fixed asset investments or capital expenditure, loan repayments and dividends to shareholders.

In general, we want to slow down cash outflows, always assuming that we are making payments on time and within agreed payment timescales and credit terms. That is the fair and honourable thing to do as we expect our customers to pay us on time and know the impact it can have if payments are delayed.

According to the 2020 QuickBooks State of Payments report, 61% of small business owners do not know how much money they spend each month.

That is a worrying statistic.

As the business owner, do you know how much money your company spends each month?

If not, why not?

You should! It is your business.

If you do not know, how can you impact it, control it, and manage it?

Clearly you cannot if you do not know.

As stated earlier, managing cash flow can be taught and mastered, and this section will help you with cash outflows.

The key difference with cash outflows compared to cash inflows is that you are in control.

You can determine whether you are making payment or not, and therefore you can control the timing of cash outflows.

Due to the lack of available funds, most small businesses tend to struggle to make payments on time. According to a recent survey on Forbes, 66% of business owners claim that delays in payment processing causes major issues with cash flow.

So, how do we better manage payments to suppliers?

PROCESS INVOICES FASTER.

As I mentioned in the Financial Management section, do everything every day. When invoices are received, they should be posted into the accounting system immediately and formally approved in some way depending upon the system you have in place. Ideally, the invoice should be matched to an already approved Purchase Order, but if not, there should be a procedure in place to ensure someone with the authority has approved an invoice before it is paid.

HAVE A SYSTEM TO COLLATE SPENDING COMMITMENTS MADE AND PURCHASES INVOICES NOT YET RECEIVED.

As stated above, a Purchase Order system works best here.

This is a system of advance approval for purchase commitments usually based on different levels of expenditure authority within the company. This allows greater control of purchases.

It also means that outstanding commitments can be considered when preparing cash flow forecasts. This is important as without it they can be missed and can have a large and detrimental impact on cash outflows depending on the nature of the business.

FOLLOW A CLEARLY DEFINED PAYMENT POLICY.

Schedule payment runs on set days. Perhaps monthly on the first day, or the first Friday of the month or something else that works for you from an administration and cash flow perspective. For some companies, a weekly payment run on a Friday may be appropriate.

This avoids situations where payments are being made daily taking up valuable administrative time and it also provides certainty from the suppliers' perspective as you build up payment patterns – they know your timings so tend to chase payment less – this again saves valuable administration time. It can also buy you a little time as your response to being chased for payment is that it will be dealt with in the next payment run rather than immediately.

REVIEW THE OUTSTANDING TRADE PAYABLES/TRADE CREDITORS SCHEDULE.

This is a great review exercise as you and your management team will become familiar with the amounts due, the key suppliers and the overall balance. Most reports will also show expenditure by supplier for the year-to-date. This information at your fingertips can be used to negotiate with suppliers to agree discounts, better payment terms or even annual retrospective discounts.

The report will also highlight any suppliers you are not paying within agreed terms and allow you to discuss with them.

UNDERSTAND YOUR DAYS PURCHASES OUTSTANDING AND THE FINANCIAL IMPACT.

This allows you to evaluate the number of days of purchases outstanding and provides an indication of how quickly you pay suppliers. If most of your credit terms are 30 days, the number should fall around this if you are paying on time. A significant lag against credit terms can be indicative of either problems with cash and the inability to pay on time or lax administrative processes.

SOME OTHER USEFUL TIPS INCLUDE:

1. If you have cash flow issues, call suppliers to discuss the challenges you are facing. Many will be very receptive to helping and deferring for a period or even agreeing to a phased payment plan. Remember that many others who owe the supplier money will ignore and avoid the issue. This puts you at a distinct advantage.
2. If you make commitments to suppliers, do not break them, particularly if payments are overdue. Do not make commitments that you cannot keep. I suggest that you call and explain that you will try to pay by a certain date depending upon your own cash inflows, and that you will follow up to confirm in advance. This allows you to build trust and develop a relationship with a specific person which can be invaluable going forward.
3. Open a "number 2 account" and transfer all employee taxes, sales taxes, and a provision for corporate taxes.
4. Stock/Inventory – understand your higher profit margin items, and analyse past sales and expected sales, and ensure you have enough, but not too much. This needs to be balanced against the time it takes to manufacture or receive from your suppliers. You do not want to lose sales, but at the same time you do not want too much cash tied up in stock that takes many weeks or even months to move. Stock/inventory needs to be reviewed regularly and the business owner must understand the stock cycle. Consider different lead times for different products. Will customers wait to receive their goods? What do your competitors do? You may also be able to have suppliers deliver more frequently and on an almost just-in-time basis.

5. When negotiating prices and credit terms with suppliers, remember that credit terms may be of more benefit to you than a lower price, especially if there are alternative suppliers of the product. This needs to be calculated and a comparison made. In times of cash challenges, I always suggest that you forego profit margin to enhance cash flow. Remember, you can renegotiate later and ask for extended credit terms and reductions in price if your sales merit it, or even in some cases if they do not. The saying "it is a buyer's market" always holds true.
6. If you have excess cash, ask for settlement discount for earlier payment. This may be appropriate if the company is forecasting excess cash and can make earlier payment than usual.
7. Negotiate an annual retrospective discount or loyalty bonus based on trading volumes and expenditure.
8. Extend payment dates to suppliers by agreement especially if there are multiple alternative suppliers. Use your status as a loyal customer who wants to stay, but needs 60 days rather than 30 days or 90 days rather than 60 days.

Remember that cash outflows are easier to forecast as they are within your control. Despite that, regular review of cash outflows is vital and must be matched against the cash inflows of the company.

We will see the importance of that more in the section on Rolling Cash Forecasts.

NEED HELP?

Knowing where to start is the most critical step in your cash flow journey. Your cash flow can best be analysed and improved with the help of a trusted adviser. I work with many companies and help them improve their cash flow.

At Know Your Numbers, we understand the difference between a thriving business and a struggling one is how well they manage their finances. When you join Know Your Numbers Mastery, you will be taught how to master your finances and how to **apply** those learnings in your business.

Make better decisions, feel more confident and less stressed, and have a thriving business.

Learn more here: **knowyournumbers.biz/**

HOW DOES THIS APPLY TO ME?

Before you move on, take a moment to reflect upon what you have learned in this chapter. What are the three most important "golden nuggets" you can apply in your business today?

_____
_____
_____
_____
_____
_____
_____
_____
_____
_____
_____
_____
_____
_____
_____
_____
_____

FINANCING GROWTH

It would be easy to write multiple books about financing growth as it is another key topic in the growth and evolution of many owner managed companies. This section strives to give you a high-level overview to help you explore this further on your own.

Many business owners have multiple opportunities, but a combination of fear and uncertainty, a lack of knowledge of how to do it and the related financial implications, as well as a lack of finances, prevents them from taking advantage of these growth opportunities.

Like many finance related problems and opportunities, the key is again (like I said in Financial Management earlier) understanding:
- where you are
- where you have been
- where you are going.

This is done by having:
- current management accounts and information, plus an up-to-date bank position – "where you are"
- historic management accounts and full year final accounts – "where you have been"
- forecasts comprising monthly profit and loss, balance sheet and cash flow as well as a weekly rolling cash flow forecast – "where you are going"

If your company is growing, your longer-term forecasts (comprising profit and loss account, balance sheet and cash flow on a monthly basis) should show the future profitability and the anticipated funding requirement going forward.

This allows you to have a discussion with banks and investors (see Banks and Investors section) and to secure the right type of finance appropriate for the type of growth you are financing.

However, the risks associated with high growth opportunities must be stressed as they can fundamentally change the risk profile of the company and the related cash requirements and profile.

A study of successful businesses conducted by Geneva Business Bank found the greatest potential threat to cash flow occurs when a company is experiencing rapid growth. During growth, a business owner usually must hire more employees, expand plant capacity, invest in capital expenditure, increase sales and customer service teams, and the operational team. Higher levels of stock or work-in-progress are usually required too.

Without proper cash flow planning this can prove to be disastrous as cash receipts generally lag all the above costs and in many cases a customer who is larger often secures longer credit terms as a condition of the growth which further exacerbates the position. For example, increasing credit terms from 30 days to 60 days. This builds higher levels of receivables outstanding and reduces the available cash for growth.

In many growth situations there is usually a build-up of physical stock and/or related work-in-progress (this is work done, but not yet completed and invoiced). This too needs to be funded and factored into the growth requirements.

As is evident, growth in the business involves a requirement for even more cash or funding solutions, and clearly this increases the risk profile of the company too.

Even more so than before it is imperative that you and your management team understand the impact of this potential growth.

There must be a clear plan outlining where the growth is coming from and how it will be managed from an operational perspective, and the costs of doing this must be clearly factored into the new financial forecasts. Can you manage it yourself or will you need to employ more management resources?

Is the growth expected to arise from more sales to existing customers, sales to new customers, additional products or services, or new geographical markets? Each has a different risk profile and potential funding requirement.

Can existing suppliers cope with your needs going forward? Do you need new suppliers and to start the trading relationship from the beginning at possibly lower credit terms? What type and how many new employees are required?

Even controlled growth creates risk and potential issues if not managed effectively, and more so, uncontrolled business growth can have a more serious detrimental impact on cash flow.

This can happen where existing customers start ordering a bit more and perhaps pull your business into providing new products and services which are an add-on to what you already provide. They are usually lower margin and not products and services that you are as familiar with. That creates more risk.

Like most things in this book this risk can be mitigated if you understand what is happening, you understand your figures, and have a clear plan and financial forecast.

Growth should not be feared, and indeed profitable growth should be embraced.

NEED HELP?

Knowing where to start is the most critical step in your cash flow journey. Your cash flow can best be analysed and improved with the help of a trusted adviser. I work with many companies and help them improve their cash flow.

At Know Your Numbers, we understand the difference between a thriving business and a struggling one is how well they manage their finances. When you join Know Your Numbers Mastery, you will be taught how to master your finances and how to **apply** those learnings in your business.

Make better decisions, feel more confident and less stressed, and have a thriving business.

Learn more here: **knowyournumbers.biz/**

HOW DOES THIS APPLY TO ME?

Before you move on, take a moment to reflect upon what you have learned in this chapter. What are the three most important "golden nuggets" you can apply in your business today?

_____
_____
_____
_____
_____
_____
_____
_____
_____

BANKS AND INVESTORS

BANKS

Banks provide loans and working capital facilities (such as overdrafts and invoice finance/factoring facilities) to many businesses.

Remember, banks only make money when lending to companies, so they are always keen to do so, but only to companies that are a good risk.

To secure bank lending, it is important to show that you and your company are a good risk.

How do you improve your chances of securing bank funding and being viewed as a good risk?

If you can tell the bank:
- Where you are
- Where you have been
- Where you are going

And you can convince them that you have an effective strategy and a good management team to deliver the operational plan, then they will lend to you all day long.

KEY TIPS:

1. Show the bank that you understand your financials and more importantly, your cash flows.
2. Show the bank that you prepare good financial information timely and regularly (historic, current, and forecast).
3. Keep the bank close to you. Share regular information, ideally share your management accounts package and updated forecasts monthly, as well as having a regular discussion perhaps quarterly.

Tell them the good news and share the bad news – but explain the bad news and what you have done about it to turn it from bad news into good news (or at least acceptable news that does not unduly worry the bank – let them know you are aware of it and are dealing with it rather than hiding from it).

WHAT TYPES OF FUNDING DO BANKS PROVIDE?

Banks can offer a variety of funding types, some of which are explained briefly below:

COMMERCIAL MORTGAGES	Used to purchase property related assets like production facilities, service depots and offices; usually repaid over 20+ years.
BUSINESS LOANS	Similar to mortgages, but not secured on property and usually based on the assets of the company and the future cash flows; usually repaid between 3 and 7 years.
ASSET FINANCE	Used to purchase assets used in the business, such as plant and machinery, production equipment, IT equipment, trucks and vans, tools and equipment, office equipment and cars; usually repaid over 3 to 5 years depending upon the asset life.
INVOICE FINANCE/ FACTORING	These facilities convert your debtor book into cash immediately usually based on a percentage of the invoice value up to 90%; great to finance growing profitable sales.
OVERDRAFT	An agreed excess cash position that the business can operate to, secured on the general assets of the company and occasionally by guarantee from the owners and directors.

Loans and asset finance facilities are repaid over a set number of years and attract an interest charge and agreement fee too, which is all agreed at the outset and before signing any documentation.

Invoice finance/factoring facilities are generally put in place for a period (e.g., 12 months and renewed annually), and attract a monthly interest charge and administration fee. Some providers also offer the ability to insure customer debts if they don't pay and that attracts an additional fee.

Banks receive their money back and make a small margin on that lending.

It is important to match the right funding to the situation that requires the financing. As outlined above there are specific types of financing and structures for different situations, and most banks will adhere closely to this.

As a business owner, it is important that you understand these structures and your obligations with respect to security, repayment and what happens if things go wrong.

Unless you have a professional and experienced adviser in your team or a part-time/fractional Chief Financial Officer (CFO) or Finance Director (FD) we encourage you to take expert advice before making any such decisions. You may also want to speak to fellow business owners and learn from their experiences.

I am an advocate of debt funding for the right situations, as it can be more appropriate and cheaper, but as mentioned above it does come with risks if you fail to repay on time.

INVESTORS

Investors are different and invest in the company by buying shares and becoming a part-owner too (shareholder). They are generally seeking longer term returns and returns that are significantly higher as they do not receive the investment money back. They are taking a bigger risk as they do not have security on assets and, as a result to balance that risk, they seek a higher return.

Their investment returns come from dividends (effectively a share of profits) and when the company is sold, just like you, so investors are often more aligned with you. It is important to discuss and agree timescales and plans before securing investment as it is vital that there is a shared goal, and timescale expectations with respect to exit and sale are aligned.

The requirements of investors are more complex and space limitations prohibits more of an explanation.

Again, it is vital to take professional financial and legal advice when considering external investment.

NEED HELP?

Knowing where to start is the most critical step in your cash flow journey. Your cash flow can best be analysed and improved with the help of a trusted adviser. I work with many companies and help them improve their cash flow.

At Know Your Numbers, we understand the difference between a thriving business and a struggling one is how well they manage their finances. When you join Know Your Numbers Mastery, you will be taught how to master your finances and how to **apply** those learnings in your business.

Make better decisions, feel more confident and less stressed, and have a thriving business.

Learn more here: **knowyournumbers.biz/**

HOW DOES THIS APPLY TO ME?

Before you move on, take a moment to reflect upon what you have learned in this chapter. What are the three most important "golden nuggets" you can apply in your business today?

_____
_____
_____
_____
_____
_____
_____
_____

KEY PERFORMANCE INDICATORS (KPIS) AND RATIOS

KPIs and ratios are largely outside the scope of this book although it would be remiss to ignore them completely.

The most important cash KPI is the cash balance and clearly the higher this is the better.

Similarly, the KPI which calculates the level of cash headroom available is also important. This KPI can be used when a company has an overdraft facility and it shows the amount of cash it is forecasting in excess of the facility limit. For example, if the cash flow shows £20,000 and the overdraft facility is £100,000 then the headroom is £120,000.

Most of the cash flow ratios are linked to the financial statements and accounts.

They compare the company's cash flows with other categories of the financial statements and accounts.

Clearly a higher level of cash flow provides business owners with greater security and confidence and provides an indication of the company's ability to suffer a decline in trading.

These ratios focus on liquidity and can provide a better indication of the financial position than the profitability of the company.

Some of these ratios include:
- **Cash flow coverage ratio:** Calculated as operating cash flows (cash flows from trading) divided by total debt. The aim is to have a high cash flow coverage ratio as it indicates that a company has sufficient cash flow to pay for scheduled principal and interest payments on any debt. The cash flow coverage ratio measures the solvency of a company and demonstrates the ability of the company to use its operating cash flows to pay off its debt.
- **Cash flow margin ratio**: Calculated as cash flow from operations divided by sales. This is a more reliable metric than net profit because it provides a clear picture of the amount of cash generated per pound/dollar of sales. This takes the cash flow timings into consideration.
- **Current liability coverage ratio**: Calculated as cash flows from operations divided by current liabilities. If this ratio is less than 1:1, a business is not generating enough cash to pay for its immediate obligations (principally trade payables/creditors) and as a result may have difficulty making such payments on time. If less than 1:1 it is usually viewed as an indicator of potential insolvency or at least cash flow issues.

Whilst such ratios are interesting and can provide insight into the trading and cash position of the company's cash flow, for most owner managed businesses, the focus on the cash position and headroom should be adequate.

NEED HELP?

Knowing where to start is the most critical step in your cash flow journey. Your cash flow can best be analysed and improved with the help of a trusted adviser. I work with many companies and help them improve their cash flow.

At Know Your Numbers, we understand the difference between a thriving business and a struggling one is how well they manage their finances. When you join Know Your Numbers Mastery, you will be taught how to master your finances and how to apply those learnings in your business.

Make better decisions, feel more confident and less stressed, and have a thriving business.

Learn more here: **knowyournumbers.biz/**

HOW DOES THIS APPLY TO ME?

Before you move on, take a moment to reflect upon what you have learned in this chapter. What are the three most important "golden nuggets" you can apply in your business today?

_____

_____

_____

_____

_____

_____

_____

_____

CASH FLOW MANAGEMENT MYTHS

This section addresses common cash flow management myths (and traps). There are many more that are used as an excuse not to manage cash flow. I suggest you ignore the myths and traps and focus on mastering cash flow.

MYTH: OUR BUSINESS IS UNIQUE; WE DO NOT NEED TO MANAGE CASH FLOW BECAUSE...

I will concede the point that your business is unique. However, if the business is to have any chance of success, you must manage cash flow. The only business that can get away without cash flow management is the rare one that has a never-ending supply of cash. To be clear, this type of business probably only became successful by focusing on cash management. For example, Apple has large cash reserves, and I guarantee that they still have a large competent team managing their cash. Be unique in who you are and what you do but embrace the power of cash flow management to succeed in business.

MYTH: MY BUSINESS IS TOO SMALL TO NEED CASH FLOW MANAGEMENT.

This is wrong, plain and simple. Business size does not determine whether your business needs cash flow management. Instead, desire for success should determine whether your business needs cash flow management. In fact, smaller businesses are often able to benefit significantly from cash flow management. Developing good habits when the company is small can have a significant impact on the business. Having a small business does not exempt you from planning or managing cash flow.

MYTH: I AM TOO BUSY TO CREATE A CASH FLOW MANAGEMENT SYSTEM.

I understand being busy. Being an entrepreneur means that we wear many hats. The key questions are:

- Are you busy working in or on your business?
- Are you working on mission critical tasks that only you can do or menial tasks that can and should be delegated?
- If you do not plan for your business' success, how will you know which tasks are mission critical?

Creating an overall plan, including cash flow management, will help you prioritise how you spend your days. Clarity from planning should reduce "busy for the sake of being busy" tasks.

Remember, you do not need to create the system. As stated in the Financial Management section earlier, bring in people to help you who understand accounts and finance either full-time, part-time or on an outsourced basis. They can build your cash flow model, or you can make use of the free gifts that I provided at the start of this book.

MYTH: I CANNOT AFFORD A CASH FLOW MANAGEMENT SYSTEM. I AM BARELY PAYING MY BILLS NOW.

You cannot afford not to. Failing to plan is planning to fail. A simple cash flow management system can be implemented easily and quickly. At its simplest, identify the bare minimum monthly expenses that your business needs to cover to survive. Once you know this, determine what sales you need to make to cover your fixed costs and any direct costs related to sales. Create a sales plan to ensure you meet this minimum number every month. Set aside surplus funds for a rainy day or start saving to make larger business purchases.

MYTH: I HAVE A SYSTEM. I WORK AS HARD AS I CAN TO EVENTUALLY PAY MY BILLS.

I am sorry to tell you this, but this is not a system and is based purely on hope and blind optimism. Hoping to pay bills "eventually" will keep you and your business trapped in survival mode. Common symptoms of this "system" include working long hours, stress, and a sense of perpetual struggle. Running out of money before you run out of month on a consistent basis is a sure sign that your current system is not working.

MYTH: I LOVE WORKING IN MY BUSINESS. I DO NOT WANT TO WASTE MY TIME WORKING ON IT.

I hear some variation of this from a lot of struggling entrepreneurs. They love creating their product or delivering their service, but do not like the stress of managing their business. Very few people are taught how to run a business while learning the skills to do the actual work of the business. If you do not want to manage your business, why are you in business? Explore what motivates you. If you truly just want to do the work, consider finding someone who can manage the business while you focus on doing the work. Remember that the cash generation capabilities of the business impact on its value. The more cash the business generates, the more it is worth.

RECAP

These are the myths that come up most often in my discussions with entrepreneurs. There are many more and far too many myths out there for me to debunk them all. If you want to find an excuse not to manage cash flow, you will.

My assumption is that by investing in this book and reading to this point that you are not looking for excuses.

As explained earlier, fear, lack of knowledge or misunderstanding can hold you back in business. You must know your numbers and you must understand your cash flow.

I expect you to act and build a successful business that focuses on cash flow. You have the tools and information to do that now, and to master cash flow.

NEED HELP?

Knowing where to start is the most critical step in your cash flow journey. Your cash flow can best be analysed and improved with the help of a trusted adviser. I work with many companies and help them improve their cash flow.

At Know Your Numbers, we understand the difference between a thriving business and a struggling one is how well they manage their finances. When you join Know Your Numbers Mastery, you will be taught how to master your finances and how to apply those learnings in your business.

Make better decisions, feel more confident and less stressed, and have a thriving business.

Learn more here: **knowyournumbers.biz/**

HOW DOES THIS APPLY TO ME?

Before you move on, take a moment to reflect upon what you have learned in this chapter. What are the three most important "golden nuggets" you can apply in your business today?

_____
_____
_____
_____

ROLLING CASH FORECASTS

Congratulations on working your way through the previous chapters. Clearly you are on your way to mastering cash flow and ensuring that you never have another sleepless night worrying about cash.

This section is where you use what you have learnt so far and aims to bring it all together in a rolling cash forecast.

The previous sections provided you with knowledge, guidance, and useful tips.

The key here is understanding the timings of cash flows and putting them all in a model together.

If you get that right, you will have become a cash flow master and the rest is easy.

As stated in the Financial Management section, a spreadsheet or workbook solution is preferable to nothing at all, but our preference is to use an online software solution with a cash management add-in, like Dryrun (**https://dryrun.com/business-owners**)
or Float (**https://floatapp.com**).
Pick a solution that is easy for you to implement and use.

At this stage do not worry too much about logistics.

You can download our free template guide here:
https://knowyournumbers.biz/downloads/.
We have provided snapshots of the template in an appendix, but the images are far less useful than the actual template.

The add-in apps will automatically populate your forecast (although you must include due and expected dates and make other assumptions/changes), so I will focus on the spreadsheet/workbook approach here.

Remember, there are three key components of a cash forecast:
1. **Cash receipts or inflows** – principally receipts from sales to customers. As a business owner and having reached this section, you already know that you should use historic data to predict future sales and timings in addition to contracts that have been agreed with customers and dates for agreed work or orders. The key is to use the best information available and to regularly review and update your assumptions and timings.
2. **Cash payments or outflows** – principally payments to suppliers and employees. Having read the section on cash inflows you will remember that cash outflows are mainly under your control, so this is always easier to forecast. Always remember to include commitments made, but not yet invoiced.
3. **Cash flow timing** – I add this as a third key component as it is the one element most often missed. This is the relationship between your cash receipts and cash payments. You should add an element of timing to your plan so that you know when to expect cash coming in and when to make outbound payments.

I want to ensure that you have visibility of the cash low points or troughs in plenty of time to do something about them. That is one of the key benefits of a rolling cash forecast and provides visibility through the 13 weeks (or the period covered by the forecast).

I also want to ensure you are maintaining cash reserves (or a working capital facility) of at least a month or two of costs.

The template workbook referred to above provides visibility for a minimum of 13 weeks or three months (it can easily be extended for more weeks – although I suggest it is not shortened below 13 weeks). Three months is generally enough time to make changes, address shortfalls and ensure adequate facilities/cash are in place to meet the demands of the business. The time frame should be long enough to be meaningful and short enough to be able to forecast reasonably accurately.

It is also suggested that you prepare some sensitivity analysis forecasts and "what if" scenarios. What if that large, expected receipt comes in a week later than forecast? What if we can move out some supplier payments for an additional week?

The hardest part of ongoing forecasting is to prepare your first model – it can take a bit of time, but please trust me as it is a worthwhile investment of time.

Generally, I start with the cash outflows as we know the timing of these is within our control.

Remember, certain payments cannot be delayed without causing significant issues:
- Employee wages and salaries – in most countries there is a legal obligation to pay these on time and in line with the employee terms of employment. If you do not pay your staff, they are unlikely to turn up for work.
- Taxation whether employee taxes, sales taxes, and corporate taxes
- Regular automated payments from your account. These are payments which come out on a specific date within the month. In the UK there are known as Standing Orders and Direct Debits or Pre-Authorised Payments in the USA and Canada.

The easiest way to start the forecast is to start with these reasonably fixed date cash outflows:
- monthly regular payments
- weekly wages
- monthly salaries
- credit card
- payroll taxes
- sales taxes
- corporate taxes

We can then factor in the receipts from customers either by inserting the total each week or using a separate worksheet that includes many customer receipts. Whatever works best for you is the recommended approach.

We then add the supplier payments on a similar basis as above.
The challenge now is once everything is populated does it show a positive or negative closing balance?

If negative, then we must look to accelerate cash inflows (usually customer receipts) or delay cash outflows (usually supplier payments).

What generally happens is that supplier payments become the balancing figure to ensure a positive position throughout, and this often means pushing them back. If done early enough we can speak to suppliers about delaying payments as discussed earlier.

Other cash inflows and outflows are factored in too and this gives us the starting point for your first rolling cash flow model.

Well done!

Remember, it is never finished as the intention is to continually monitor it and update it with new information. It is a dynamic model and should become the key report you use in the company to manage cash flow.

Every week I recommend that one week is added at the end and the earliest week is updated for the actual results. Then a detailed weekly review should be carried out and a variance report prepared showing the actual result against the previous forecast. Perform a variance analysis on the prior week's actual numbers and understand why it was different, and more importantly understand the impact going forward and adjust the forecast accordingly

The rolling nature of the forecast is because we remove one week and add another week. This allows the future weeks to be updated if say receipts slipped a few days into another week or we had to delay supplier payments as a result.

Ask questions and check key assumptions, especially large inflows and outflows. The phrase "trust but verify" is a good way to look at it.

What was different from forecast last week? Did a large customer payment not come in? Are we confident that it will come in next week? Have we checked with our customer?

The rolling cash flow model is great to understand and predict the impact of difficult months perhaps due to a seasonal downturn or perhaps the sales tax due quarter.

The key to cash flow forecasting is to be aware of shortfalls early.

OTHER USEFUL TIPS:

1. Remember to factor in seasonality of sales. If your business has seasonal peaks and troughs, you need to be aware of this and factor it into your planning.
2. I mentioned debtor days and creditor days in earlier sections – as a business owner you need to fund the gap between the difference in these. For example, if you collect your inflows in 47 days and must pay your creditors in 30 days (as well as paying employees at the end of every week and/or month) this can be a challenge. It is vital to stay on top of this.
3. Track and monitor daily.
4. Be conservative in forecasting – I always like to err on the conservative side with cash inflows and build in some "slack" and at the same time assume my payments are made a bit earlier than required. Be realistic. This means that your business has some contingency already built in and will help you avoid unexpected surprises.

The accuracy of forecasting should be reviewed regularly. As advised above I suggest that the weekly rolling cash flow is analysed every week. We need to compare the previous week forecast with the actual outcome. The actual outcome is updated, and another week added to the end of the forecast. This keeps it dynamic.

We want to understand:
- What are we forecasting well?
- What are we forecasting badly?
- Are there any regular challenges that keep arising?
- Do we have the same customers making late payments or failing to deliver on promises?

This allows us to make changes and act early.

NEED HELP?

Knowing where to start is the most critical step in your cash flow journey. Your cash flow can best be analysed and improved with the help of a trusted adviser. I work with many companies and help them improve their cash flow.

At Know Your Numbers, we understand the difference between a thriving business and a struggling one is how well they manage their finances. When you join Know Your Numbers Mastery, you will be taught how to master your finances and how to **apply** those learnings in your business.

Make better decisions, feel more confident and less stressed, and have a thriving business.

Learn more here: **knowyournumbers.biz/**

HOW DOES THIS APPLY TO ME?

Before you move on, take a moment to reflect upon what you have learned in this chapter. What are the three most important "golden nuggets" you can apply in your business today?

_____
_____
_____
_____
_____
_____
_____
_____
_____
_____
_____
_____
_____
_____
_____
_____
_____

THE NEXT STEP

Thank you and congratulations for working through my book. Celebrate this as a victory as you now know more about cash flow than the majority of your fellow entrepreneurs! I hope I have been able to share helpful information that you can apply in your business today.

I know you are probably feeling a mixture of fear and excitement about the next step in your journey. I would be honoured to help you and guide you on your business journey. I am here for you; you are not alone.

Thank you for your time, and if I can be of service to you, please reach out to me at:

craig@knowyournumbers.biz

APPENDICES

1. Cash Flow Diagnostic
2. Recommended Reading
3. KYN Training Academy
4. Rolling Cash Flow
5. Case Studies

1) CASH FLOW DIAGNOSTIC

I have created a simple diagnostic tool to help you understand the cash flow risk that's inherent in your business. It only takes a couple of minutes but will give you an incredibly valuable insight into your business.

You can take the diagnostic at:

kyncashflowdiagnostic.com

2) RECOMMENDED READING

Pandemic Cash Flow: Cash flow issues kill nearly 30% of businesses. Why it happens, and how to prevent it by **Blaine Bertsch**

Profit First: Transform Your Business from a Cash-Eating Monster to a Money-Making Machine by **Mike Michalowicz**

Financial Foreplay: Whip Your Business into Shape - Take Home More Cash by **Rhondalynn Korolak**

3) KYN TRAINING ACADEMY

Learn how to make better decisions.

We have created short training videos to help you understand the key principles of the Know Your Numbers Framework and to teach you how to improve your overall business acumen.

**Access them here:
knowyournumbers.biz/kyn-training-academy**

4) ROLLING CASH FLOW EXAMPLE

Below is an example of a cash flow template; you can download our cash flow template here:
https://knowyournumbers.biz/downloads

The summary

COMPANY NAME
13 Week Rolling Cashflow
Week Commencing 1st January 2024
Summary

Week Commencing		01/01/24	08/01/24	15/01/24...
		Actual		
Opening Balance	Note 1	0	0	0
Receipts				
Customer Receipts		0	0	0
HMRC VAT refund		0	0	0
Loans/Grants Received		0	0	0
Number 2 Account		0	0	0
Other		0	0	0
Total Receipts		0	0	0
Payments				
Supplier Payments		0	0	0
Direct Debits / Standing Orders		0	0	0
Weekly salaries (ADD DAY PAID)		0	0	0
Monthly salaries (ADD DAY PAID)		0	0	0
Credit Card (limit XXX) - DATE		0	0	0
PAYE/NIC - monthly (ADD DATE)		0	0	0
VAT (ADD DATE/MONTH/QUARTER)		0	0	0
Corporation (ADD DATE)		0	0	0
Capital Expenditure		0	0	0
Dividends		0	0	0
Number 2 Account		0	0	0
Other		0	0	0
Total Payments		0	0	0
Net Cash Inflow / (Outflow)		0	0	0
Closing Balance	Note 1	- 0	0	0
Overdraft Facility		0	0	0
Surplus / (Deficit)		0	0	0

Customer Receipts

COMPANY NAME
13 Week Rolling Cashflow
Week Commencing 1st January 2024
Customer Receipts

Customer	01/01/24	08/01/24	15/01/24...
Customer 1			
Customer 2			
etc			
etc			
	0	0	0

Supplier Payments

COMPANY NAME
13 Week Rolling Cashflow
Week Commencing 1st January 2024
Supplier Payments

	01/01/24	08/01/24	15/01/24...
Supplier 1			
Supplier 2			
etc			
etc			
	0	0	0

Direct Debits and Standing Orders

COMPANY NAME
13 Week Rolling Cashflow
Week Commencing 1st January 2024
Direct Debits and Standing Orders

Date	Amount	Payee	Ends	Description	01/01/24	08/01/24	15/01/24...
Fixed							
		#1					
		#2					
		#3					
		etc					
	0.00				0.00	0.00	0.00
Variable							
		#1					
		#2					
		etc					
	0.00				0.00	0.00	0.00
Quarterly							
		#1					
		etc					
	0.00				0.00	0.00	0.00
	0.00				0.00	0.00	0.00

5) CASE STUDIES

CASE STUDY #1: MANAGING AND FINANCING SIGNIFICANT GROWTH, AND A REDUCTION IN STRESS

I was introduced to the directors of a rapidly growing business by their existing bank. The bank wanted to support the growth plans of the business owner but were unable to as the financial information was poor.

Turnover had more than doubled in the previous financial year and the company was annualising another 100% plus increase. This was putting significant pressure on cash flow and the business owner and his team were experiencing significant growing pains as a result.

This was creating stress, worry, a strain on personal and professional relationships, and many sleepless nights. Cash was extremely tight, and the business was clearly over-trading based on its existing banking facilities. Supplier credit limits were causing a difficulty as they were based on the filed historical accounts when the company was less than half of its current size.

Many customers were lax in paying within the company's credit terms and there was a potential problem with several significantly overdue trade debtors. Whilst credit terms were 30 days, the average debtor days outstanding were over 80.

There was no experienced finance professional within the business and the external accountants provided only statutory and historic support.

I worked closely with the directors and company's finance providers; I performed an Initial Project covering the following key areas:
- detailed review of the company's suppliers and credit limits.
- detailed review of the customer base and outstanding balances due.
- finalisation of the prior year accounts to enable filing at Companies House.
- assistance in the preparation of the weekly rolling cash flow forecast.
- assistance in the preparation of the current year budget including profit and loss, balance sheet and cash flow.

As part of the Project, we met with the company's finance providers and told them the changes we had already implemented and our plans for going forward. By increasing their confidence, we secured an almost doubling of the working capital facility.

In addition, we engaged with the key suppliers and secured increases in credit limits and credit terms.

I worked with the business owner and the internal team to create a detailed action plan with respect to the amounts outstanding from customers.

We increased the finance support internally by recruiting an experienced credit controller and she assisted in implementing our new way of engaging with customers and collection of the older debts. This was mainly done by speaking to the customer, resolving issues, and explaining how we would be operating going forward.

The ageing profile and debtors' days figures are already showing vast improvements.

The directors were aware of their lack of experience in certain key areas and addressed this by making changes with my ongoing assistance.

The business owner now spends significantly less time worrying about cash and can meet all his obligations to suppliers and employees as they fall due. His stress level reduced significantly and there are no longer sleepless nights worrying about cash flow.

CASE STUDY #2: IMPROVED FINANCIAL MANAGEMENT, NEW BANK FACILITIES, AND AN END TO SLEEPLESS NIGHTS

I was introduced to a company that had extremely poor financial information and had suffered from poor internal and external financial support.

The family-owned company had almost doubled turnover in the prior year and were annualising another significant increase in the current year. However, financial information was significantly behind where it should be and that which was available appeared to be not only out-of-date, but wholly inaccurate.

The first phase of our role involved three main elements:
- Review of Existing Financial Management and Reporting
- Review of Cash Management and Forecasting
- Preparation of the Budget

As part of the process new accounting advisers were appointed and we worked closely with them to ensure that the previous year end figures and balance sheet were accurate, to allow that as a starting point and basis for going forward.

Internal roles and responsibilities were changed, and various new reports and controls were introduced.

As a result of the changes, the new team, and significantly better information, we engaged with the bank who agreed to increase the existing finance facilities to allow the company to finance its growth plans.

The new reporting regime generates timely and accurate information produced on a weekly and monthly basis, and it is formally reviewed by the board at the monthly meeting. The rolling 13-week cash flow model is updated weekly and used as a basis for managing cash and making key investment decisions going forward.

The owner is delighted with the new information and can now sleep soundly at night.

The additional benefits of the changes have been an improvement in gross margin, a greater control over cash, and greater certainty over historic results and the way forward. The revised strategy which we have assisted in developing has seen the company consider an acquisition, plan for future investment, and consider longer-term succession.

I continued to support the company in a part-time Finance Director role to oversee the financial management of the company and it is now well placed for continued profitable growth over the next few years, and a planned and phased exit by the business owner.

CASE STUDY #3: CHANGED REPORTING CULTURE PRODUCES MILLIONS IN NEW FUNDING AND HUGE GROWTH IN PROFITS

I was introduced to the directors of a business with significant growth potential.

The business had shown strong growth over several years, but this had stalled because of poor financial management and a resulting lack of confidence from the bank and other funders. The lack of growth finance meant that the company could not take advantage of the numerous opportunities from existing customers and new potential customers.

I performed an "Initial Review" exercise over a few days and identified several key areas that required improvement. I was invited by the shareholders to work with the management team to effect these changes.

As part of my role, I worked closely with the bank and other potential funders to identify the changes required to improve their confidence, thereby allowing the provision of the working capital facilities and other asset finance facilities required to deliver the growth opportunities. I also worked closely with the operational team, to identify the information required to run the business from their perspective.

I improved the reporting culture within the company, altered the roles and responsibilities of the finance team members and recruited two new staff to assist in the process. The improvement in the revised information allowed more effective internal reporting and a greater understanding of the business, from a profitability and cash flow basis. The revised financial reports that the bank received on an ongoing basis provided them with the key information they required, and over the course of several months the bank continued to increase facilities on an "as required" basis to finance growth.

The budget for the current financial year was updated to reflect the changes and the opportunities that the company was now able to deliver.

A greater focus was placed on cash and cash collection, and a rolling cash flow model was introduced alongside weekly "cash" team meetings. Debtor days were reduced significantly, and the new information was used to "run the business".

The company operated with this reorganised structure and this benefited all parties with performance ahead of a demanding budget, and a new corporate and professional approach from a finance perspective.

I provided ongoing support through a part-time Finance Director role and became the key point of contact for the bank. This worked well for all parties and allowed the operational management team to focus on "running the business".

This Case Study shows strength of having good financial information and working closely with the bank as without it the company would have been unable to take advantage of the significant growth opportunities.

ABOUT THE AUTHOR
CRAIG ALEXANDER RATTRAY

Craig Alexander Rattray is a Scottish Chartered Accountant, entrepreneur, growth strategist, and cash flow expert.

He has worked in various fields ranging from accountancy, private equity, venture capital, and corporate finance, to business strategy, and industrial financial management. He is the founder of CR Corporate Solutions (Craig Alexander Rattray Limited) and various other early stage and high-growth companies, and operates a group coaching/teaching initiative Know Your Numbers (www.knowyournumbers.biz). He has assisted multiple university start-ups and early-stage companies to develop strategy, build a team, create direction, raise finance, and leverage financial management.

His current focus is working with a portfolio of growing ambitious companies and leading them on their journey from six figures and beyond to multiple millions and hosting various Know Your Numbers groups.

He started his Chartered Accountancy training contract with Arthur Andersen in 1991, but has never seen himself as an accountant. His focus has always been forward looking and working with clients to increase profitability, enhance cashflow and build shareholder value.

Craig Alexander wrote this book to show that cashflow management is not difficult and to give the typical business owner the knowledge and practical advice to become a cashflow master.

GLOSSARY

BUDGET

A budget is an estimation of revenue and expenses over a specified future period of time and is usually compiled and re-evaluated on a periodic basis. Budgets can be made for a person, a family, a group of people, a business, a government, a country, a multinational organisation or just about anything else that makes and spends money. At companies and organisations, a budget is an internal tool used by management and is often not required for reporting by external parties.

CASH FLOW

Cash flow is the net amount of cash that an entity receives and disburses during a period. Quite simply, cash flow is the flow of cash into and out of your business bank account.

CASH INFLOW

Cash inflow is the money going into a business. That could be from sales, loans, grants, investment, or financing. It is the opposite of cash outflow.

CASH FLOW MANAGEMENT

The process of planning a company's schedule for paying bills and estimating when income is likely to be received. Cash flow management helps a company avoid damaging its relationship with creditors, employees, and the government by not paying bills on time and being forced into insolvency.

CASH OUTFLOW

Cash outflow is the money leaving the business. A business is usually considered healthy if its cash inflow is greater than its cash outflow.

FORECASTING

Forecasting is the process of making predictions of the future based on past and present data and most commonly by analysis of trends. A commonplace example might be estimation of some variable of future sales based on historic trends and order book.

KEY PERFORMANCE INDICATORS

A Key Performance Indicator (KPI) is a measurable value that demonstrates how effectively a company is achieving key business objectives. Organisations use KPIs at multiple levels to evaluate performance, trends, and general health of the business.

PROFIT

Profit is a financial gain, generally the difference between the amount earned and the amount spent in buying, operating, or producing something. Quite simply, profit is the difference between the total of all sales less the total of all costs and expenses for a particular period.

ROLLING FORECAST

A rolling forecast is an add/drop process for predicting the future over a set period. In our template example the rolling forecast is for 13 weeks. After the first week is completed, that week is dropped, and another added at the end of the forecast. A rolling forecast requires routine revisions, and is sometimes referred to as a continuous forecast or an iterative forecast.

Printed in Great Britain
by Amazon